Holiday Fun
Painting Christmas Gourds

Sammie Crawford,
The Fairy Gourdmother®

Schiffer Publishing Ltd

4880 Lower Valley Road · Atglen, PA · 19310

Other Schiffer Books by Sammie Crawford
Gourd Fun (for everyone), 978-0-7643-3124-4, $22.99

Other Schiffer Books on Related Subjects
Making Gourd Ornaments, 978-0-7643-2716-2, $12.95
Gourd Crafts: 6 Projects & Patterns, 978-0-7643-2825-1, $14.95
Decorating Gourds: Carving, Burning, Painting & More, 0-7643-1312-6, $14.95

Disclaimer
Because of the unique nature of gourds, these patterns may have to be altered to fit each individual gourd. You may enlarge, shrink, or alter them any way necessary to make them work for you.

Schiffer Books are available at special discounts for bulk purchases for sales promotions or premiums. Special editions, including personalized covers, corporate imprints, and excerpts can be created in large quantities for special needs. For more information contact the publisher:

Published by Schiffer Publishing Ltd.
4880 Lower Valley Road
Atglen, PA 19310
Phone: (610) 593-1777; Fax: (610) 593-2002
E-mail: Info@schifferbooks.com

For the largest selection of fine reference books on this and related subjects, please visit our web site at:
www.schifferbooks.com
We are always looking for people to write books on new and related subjects. If you have an idea for a book please contact us at the above address.

This book may be purchased from the publisher.
Include $5.00 for shipping.
Please try your bookstore first.
You may write for a free catalog.

In Europe, Schiffer books are distributed by
Bushwood Books
6 Marksbury Ave.
Kew Gardens
Surrey TW9 4JF England
Phone: 44 (0) 20 8392 8585; Fax: 44 (0) 20 8392 9876
E-mail: info@bushwoodbooks.co.uk
Website: www.bushwoodbooks.co.uk

Acknowledgments

A thanks goes out to all the people who encouraged me to do this book.

A special thanks to Jim Widess at the Caning Shop in Berkeley, California, for putting me in touch with Schiffer Publishing. Without him, I doubt this book would exist.

Thanks to my editor, Tina Skinner, Doug Congdon-Martin, and all the fine folks at Schiffer Publishing who helped make this book a reality.

Dedication

This book is dedicated to my wonderful husband of 42 years, Harry. All I am I owe to him. He has encouraged me in anything I wanted to try, never once questioning my ability to do it. While he is my biggest fan, he is also my harshest critic. I know I can depend on him to tell me the truth even if it hurts a tad. At least I know he's usually right and I depend on that, too. Thanks, love, for all you do.

Copyright © 2009 by Sammie Crawford
Library of Congress Control Number: 2009926159

Designed by RoS
Type set in Formal436 BT/NewBskvll BT

ISBN: 978-0-7643-3279-1
Printed in China

Contents

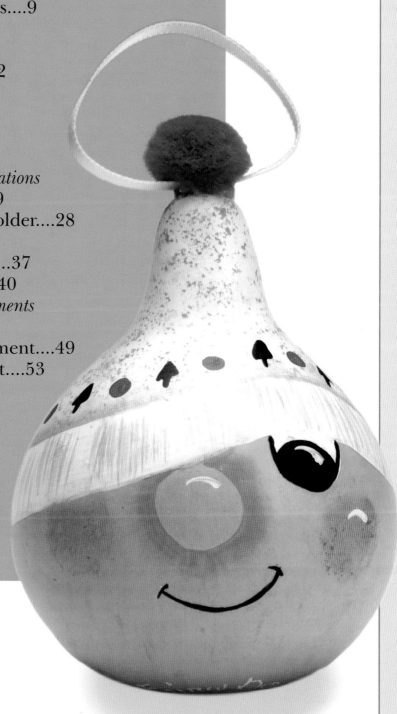

A Short History
of the Gourd

People often ask how long a gourd will last. If you use it outside for something such as a birdhouse, it won't last more than a few years even though it is painted. The Martin houses you see are taken down every year, cleaned out, and repainted, but they still don't hold up. However, if gourds are kept in a protected area out of the weather, they probably won't last more than a couple of thousand years. Gourds have been found in caves that dated back to 2000 B.C. with traces of grains still stored in them.

As a relative of pumpkins and squash, they are found anywhere these crops can be grown. However, in tropical zones there is a gourd that grows not on a vine but on a tree and is found in places like Africa, the Virgin Islands, and Hawaii. It is the Calabash and gets as large as a basketball. I'm sure the natives know not to walk under that tree. (*Actually, they grow on the trunk.*)

People worldwide have always known the value of gourds, using them for everything from storage vessels to masks for frightening away evil spirits in religious ceremonies, to decorative clothing, noisemakers and musical instruments, utensils, toys, trade items, money, pipes, and even as pesticides and in enrichment programs at zoos. Today they are a thriving industry due to the fact that they have become so popular as a painting surface with crafters and artists.

In the Southwest a gourd called the Coyote or Buffalo gourd grows wild in the arroyos of the desert. The local natives crushed these gourds and soaked them in water; creating a smelly pesticide they put on their crops to repel insects. I've also been told that they used the large Zucca gourds as caskets for infants and small children.

I recently learned that in certain parts of the Hindu religion, they believe that Noah survived the Great Flood not by building an ark but by putting everyone inside a giant gourd and floating away. I found this hard to believe until I met an Indian and was able to confirm that it is, indeed, true. That must have truly been one bodacious gourd!

When I began painting gourds about fifteen years ago, the only one I was familiar with was the dipper gourd that always hung by my grandmother's well. I had no idea that there were different kinds and they all had names. I thought you planted a seed and whatever you got was a surprise shape-wise. I didn't know that if you wanted cannonballs, you planted cannonball seeds and if you wanted kettles, you planted kettle seeds. I now know the names of twenty-five different shapes and I'm still learning. Gourd growers country wide have tried to standardize the names so that someone on the

<4>

west coast will know which one someone on the east coast is talking about. And gourd farms have become big business in the last few years because the gourds' wonderfully smooth surfaces have been "discovered" by the crafters and artists.

I tried growing my own gourds the first year that I painted them, but I quickly learned that it was farming—and farming is a lot like work. I wasted no time in locating a gourd farm, but I have to tell you about that first crop. I knew less than nothing about gourds. After a summer of minimal results — I think I had a dozen undersized gourds — I was watching the weather report when they announced there would be a frost that night. I flew into a panic and my husband and I went outside in our nighties and slippers, gathering in our "crop." We couldn't figure out where to put the little darlings to protect them until hubby said we should put them in the garage and he would connect a light to keep them warm. You would have thought we were raising baby chicks!

Not long after that, I visited my first gourd farm and saw thousand of gourds lying out in the open on wooden pallets. I asked the farmer what he did to protect them when it frosted or rained. He said, "Lady, it snows on 'em. It ain't gonna hurt 'em." I did not tell him about my crop.

Are you surprised that there are gourd farms and that people actually raise gourds *on purpose*? Here's another surprise for you. There is an American Gourd Society. It is headquartered in Mt. Gilead, Ohio, and almost every state has at least one chapter or "gourd patch" as they are called. These chapters are filled with not just artists, but people who can't even paint. They just like to raise gourds and if you ask them or anyone associated with gourds why they like them, rarely will the answer be anything other than "I don't know. I just like them."

The gourd that is most popular with artists is the hardshell; it's different from those pretty multi-colored ornamental gourds you see in the markets in the fall. They bear a white flower that blooms at night as opposed to the ornamental's yellow blossom that blooms in the day. The hardshell dries dependably and the ornamental is more likely to rot. And the hardshells get much, much larger.

Be sure to give your gourd vines lots of room and sunshine. Their growth habits are like their relatives— watermelons, squash, and pumpkins. They also require a lot of water in order to produce nice, thick shells.

The vine bears both male and female blooms. When the vine reaches five or six feet, pinch off the tips back to the first or second set of leaves. This forces the lateral growth and that is where the female blooms are located. This will produce a lot more gourds than if you didn't pinch it off.

Provide a trellis or fence for the vines if you want the gourds like dippers to be nice and straight. The weight of the gourd pulls them straight. If allowed to grow on the ground, they will have wonderful, curly handles.

If you intend to grow more than one variety and want to use the seeds from one crop for the next one, you must keep the

<5>

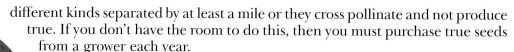

different kinds separated by at least a mile or they cross pollinate and not produce true. If you don't have the room to do this, then you must purchase true seeds from a grower each year.

They need to be planted as soon as danger of frost has passed since they have a long growing season. In the fall, do not harvest them until the first frost has killed the vine and the stems have turned brown. If you harvest before this, the odds are that your crop will rot rather than dry. If you don't have a good place to dry them, leaving them hanging on the vine through the winter is an option. However, if you are in an area that freezes and intend to use the seeds, they will not germinate as well as seeds that haven't frozen. If you do harvest them, place them somewhere where they get sun and the air can circulate around them. I have a place where I can make a chicken wire "hammock" for them, but be careful. I loaded so many into the hammock that I almost pulled a chain link fence down with the weight. They may weigh nothing when dry, but they are equal in weight to a watermelon of that size when green.

People often ask me how you make a gourd dry. You don't. They do it on their own and, in fact, you can't stop them. This is a natural process they go through. They are 98% water and all that water will evaporate through the shell to dry. Don't drill holes in them to speed up the drying process. This only opens the door for bacteria and pests to enter and ruin your gourds.

During that process, they will turn black and moldy. It is at this point that most first time growers throw them away, thinking that they're ruined. DON'T DO THAT. Once they are dry, they will be very lightweight and the seeds usually rattle. Now it's time to take them in the house and clean them.

Run several inches of water in the sink, add a few ounces of bleach, and let the gourds float around and soak for five or ten minutes. Use a plastic scrubber pad to remove most of the mold. The few stubborn spots can be removed with a dull paring knife. Get them completely clean because any mold left on can come loose later and take your paint with it.

Let them dry overnight or, if you're in a hurry, put them in the oven on the lowest setting for 20-30 minutes. Then you're ready to paint.

Gourds do not require a sealer before painting like wood does and I like the fact that there is no sanding or sealing prep work. I use acrylic paint and a spray varnish. In recent years I have begun to "sculpt" the gourds, cutting out shapes and gluing them to another gourd to create different things. They are truly a wonderful medium to work with. In fact I haven't found anything I can't do with a gourd except perhaps eat it. It's amazing to me that a growing thing with no food value has lasted so long down through the ages and been so indispensable to so many for so many reasons. It makes you look at gourds in an entirely different light, doesn't it?

I highly recommend joining both the American Gourd Society, 317 Maple Court, Kokomo, Indiana 46902-3633, and the Society of Decorative Painters, 393 McLean Boulevard, Wichita, Kansas 67203-5968. Both of these organizations deserve your support and you will benefit greatly from the association

<6>

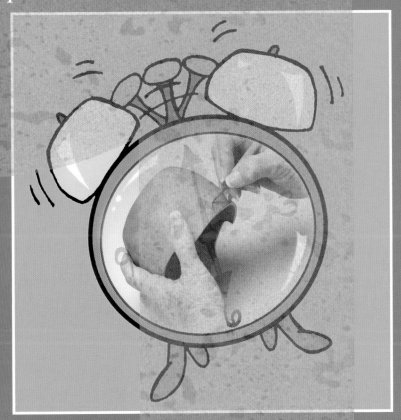

part ONE

Getting Started

Your Tools

Tools Used in this Book

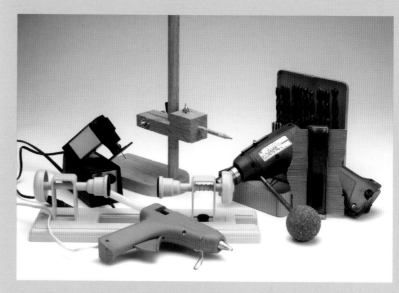

From left: Craft saw, craft lathe, glue gun, leveling marker, drill and bits, profile tool, and gourd cleaning tool.

Your Supplies

Supplies Used in this Book

From left: Gourd and plywood scraps, X-Acto knife, music box, pompoms, spray varnish, narrow ribbon, acrylic stars, wood glue, wooden heads, spackle, craft glue, and painter's tape.

<8>

Gourd Identification Chart

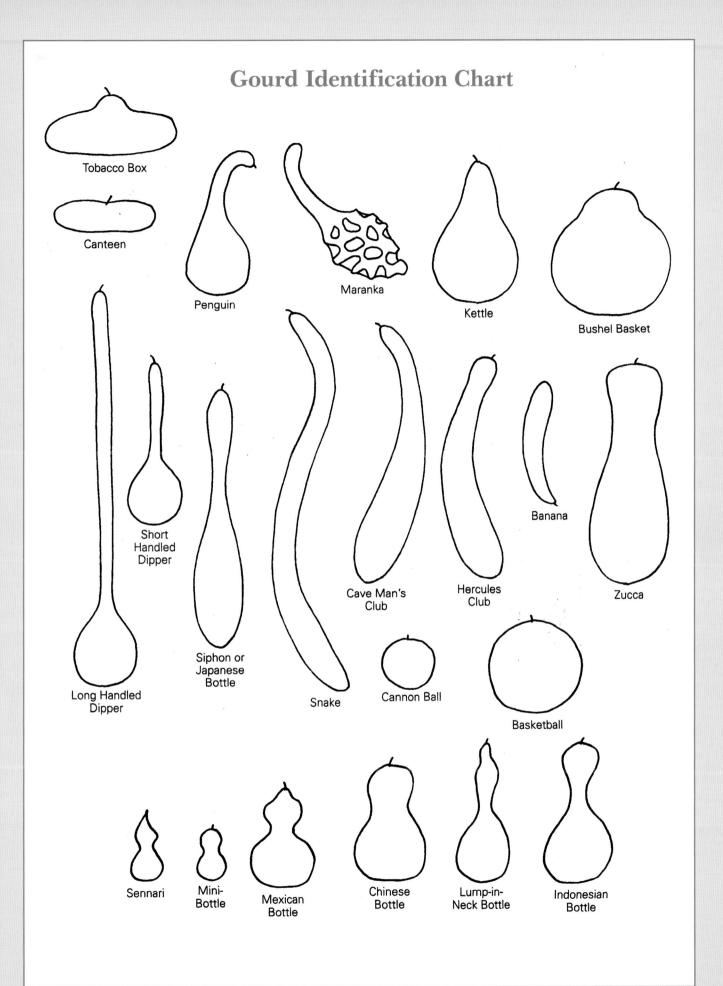

Tobacco Box

Canteen

Penguin

Maranka

Kettle

Bushel Basket

Short Handled Dipper

Long Handled Dipper

Siphon or Japanese Bottle

Snake

Cave Man's Club

Hercules Club

Banana

Zucca

Cannon Ball

Basketball

Sennari

Mini-Bottle

Mexican Bottle

Chinese Bottle

Lump-in-Neck Bottle

Indonesian Bottle

<9>

Gourd Sources

The projects in this book were painted on a variety of gourd shapes, all of which are readily available from any gourd farm. Most farms have websites where you can see the shapes and prices before ordering. Some farms don't sell dirty gourds, but the ones who do offer them at a slightly lower price than the clean ones. They will ship anywhere usually without a minimum order.

My source for gourds is Dalton Farms, 610 CR 336, Piggott, AR 72454. Their website is www.pumpkinhollow.com and their phone number is 870-598-3568. You will enjoy doing business with Ellen Dalton.

<10>

*part*TWO:

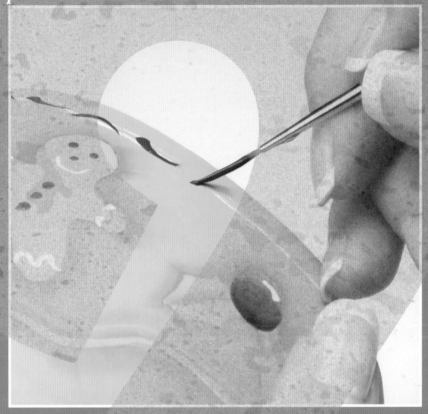

Painting Gourds

Gourd Painting Tips

TIP #1

When choosing dirty gourds, pick the blackest, dirtiest gourds with the most mold you can find. I've learned that the pretty, clean, light-colored ones are ten times harder to clean than the black ones so the nastier, the better.

During the drying process, the moisture coming out through the skin produces mold. This is what loosens the skin and makes it easier to clean.

TIP #2

You can tell by the weight of gourds which ones have thick shells. Try to pick the heaviest ones you can find. Thin-shelled gourds are more easily broken if dropped or when being cut.

TIP #3

When using a sponge, **never** wring it out. Squeeze to remove excess water and if you want it drier, roll it in a paper towel and squeeze again.

TIP #4

If you begin to run out of color when pouncing with a sponge, don't mash harder. This just blurs or muddies your color. Go back to the paint and refill the sponge

TIP #5

Never let paint reach the ferrule (metal) on your brush. Once it gets inside, it's extremely hard to remove and reduces the life of your brush. Instead, rinse the brush and reload. Nowhere is it written that what you are painting must be done in one fell swoop!

TIP #6

Got ridges down the sides of your brush stroke? You're overloading your brush. Several light coats of paint are much better than one heavy coat. They also dry faster and look more professional when free of those ridges.

TIP #7

The easiest way to apply a flat pattern to a round object is to cut the pattern into pieces. Separate the doors, windows, etc. on a cottage and apply the individual features where needed. You can do it!

<12>

TIP #8

To get the best streak-free coverage with Gold, undercoat with a light tan or brown first.

TIP #9

Always keep damp Q-tips handy to erase mistakes. I have found nothing that works better. A damp Q-tip will erase most pattern lines, too.

TIP #10

When painting on dark surfaces, always undercoat reds, yellows, and other transparent colors with white.

TIP #11

Always use paint thinned to the consistency of ink when using a liner brush. If it isn't thinned, the paint doesn't flow from the brush.

TIP #12

Never hold a liner brush like a pencil or lean it. Holding it straight up and down will get you the beautiful desired thin lines you want.

TIP #13

When using a liner brush to make flowing vines and tendrils, put your entire arm into the process and let the motion flow from your shoulder. If you only depend on the motion of your hand and wrist, you may wind up with cramped, irregular shaky lines.

TIP #14

Fill eyes in completely with solid white first. This makes it easier to see that they are the same size, level, and evenly spaced on the face.

Final Thoughts

All brushes suggested for these projects are just that — suggestions. You must use the brush size that fits the space best and feels best for you.

When it comes to brushes, there are two points I am very firm on.

1. Always clean your brushes well and lay them flat to dry. NEVER stand a wet brush on end. You may think it's clean, but if there is even a trace of paint left in it, where do you think it will go when you stand it up? Into the ferrule and soon your brushes look like they have stuck their little bristles in a light socket! Another useless brush.

2. NEVER leave a brush standing in water, not even "just to answer the phone." The handle will absorb water and swell. When it dries out and shrinks, the ferrule will be loose and fall right off the handle. It's hard to paint without a handle.

<13>

Painting Stroke Illustrations

In each of these three stroke illustrations, you will be using water to thin paint. This is the only time you will add water to your paints for the projects in this book.

Floating or Side-loading a Brush

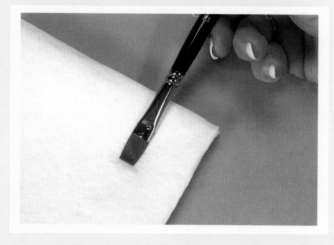

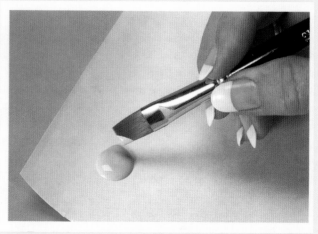

1 Use at least a #12 or 1/2" wide brush. Moisten the brush with clean water and blot on a paper towel just until it loses its sheen. Leave as much water without it being drippy.

2 Holding it at a 45-degree angle, dip the corner of the brush in the paint.

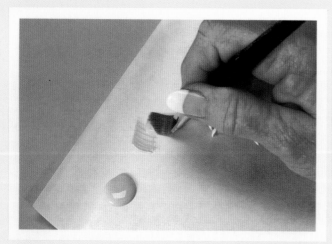

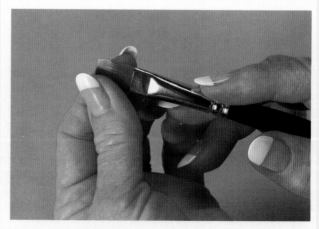

3 Apply a slight pressure and work the brush back and forth on the palette. Be careful not to let the paint get on the clean side of the brush.

4 Flip the brush over and gently pinch off the water from the brush. Some people don't do this, but I find I have a "halo" along the edge of my float if I don't.

<14>

Using a Liner Brush

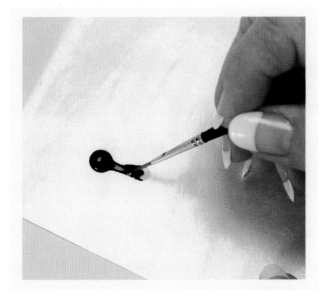

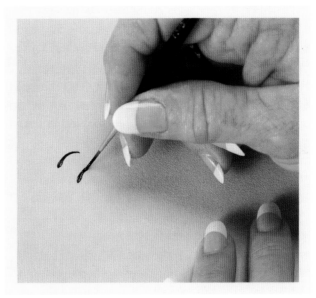

1 When using a liner brush, always thin the paint to the consistency of milk or ink. Do this by pulling a small amount of paint over to a drop of water on your palette. *(If you don't thin it, the paint will not flow off the brush tip.)*

2 When the brush is dressed, pull the point back in shape by rotating the brush between your fingers as you pull it across the palette. Regular liners are fine for comma strokes, but if you are making long lines, try using a script liner.

Using Your Rake Brush

1 Moisten your brush and blot on a paper towel just until it loses its shine. Dress the brush with paint and work it back and forth on the palette. Set the brush down on the palette and fan the bristles by applying slight pressure and rotating the brush between your fingers. But don't let the metal ferrule touch because it can cut the bristles off.

2 If you have the correct amount of water and paint in your brush, light strokes will produce fine lines. Too much or too little water and it makes a solid stroke. It's just a matter of practice. Once you find the balance, you will really enjoy making hair, beards, and fur.

<15>

*part*THREE:

The Projects

Musical Snow Globe

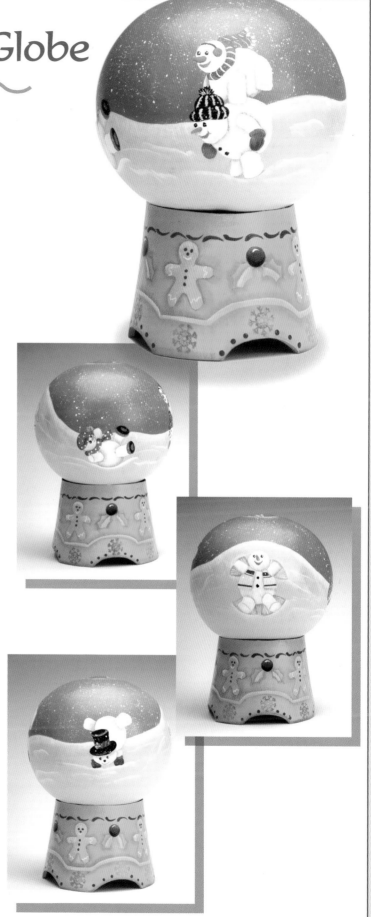

Palette – Delta Ceramcoat

Roman Stucco • Mocha • Ivory
• Black Cherry • White • Black
• Deep Coral • Cape Cod Blue
•Chambray Blue • Deep River
Green • Opaque Red
• Bittersweet

Brushes – Loew-Cornell

Series 7300 #12 flat
Series 7350 10/0 liner
Series 7500 #6 filbert
Series 7550 1" wash brush
515-L berry maker
275 mop

Supplies

3" section of 4" diameter club
gourd
5-6" diameter cannonball gourd
Wood glue
Craft saw* or craft knife
Snowflake stamp
Wind-up music box**
¼" plywood scrap, 5" sq.
Drill and bits
Delta spray varnish

*The craft saw is available from tur-
tlefeathers.net 1-828-488-8586
**The music box is available from
Klockit.com 1-800-556-2548

<19>

REPEAT PATTERN TO
ENCIRCLE BASE

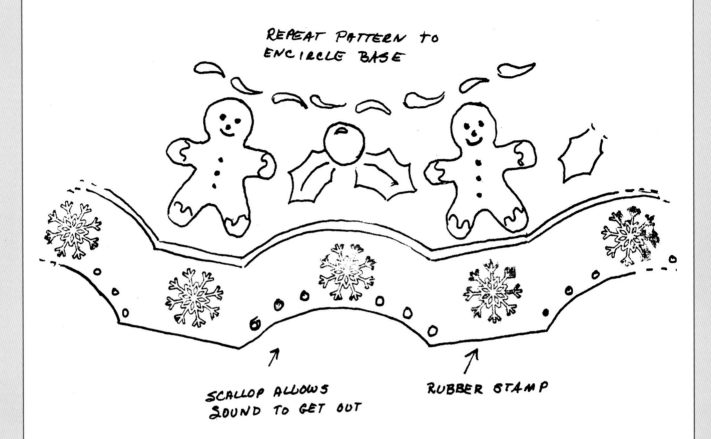

SCALLOP ALLOWS
SOUND TO GET OUT

RUBBER STAMP

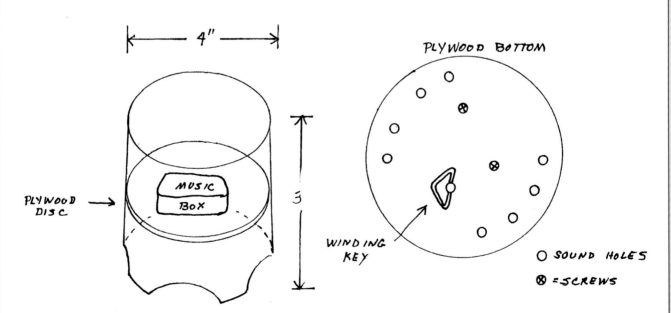

4"

PLYWOOD
DISC →

MUSIC
BOX

3

PLYWOOD BOTTOM

WINDING
KEY

○ SOUND HOLES
⊗ = SCREWS

THERE MUST BE SPACE AT THE BOTTOM FOR THE KEY TO CLEAR
AND SPACE AT THE TOP FOR THE CANNONBALL TO SEAT & BE
GLUED.

<20>

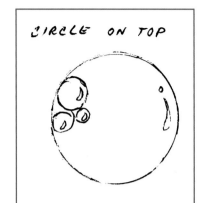

CIRCLE ON TOP

<21>

Building the Music Box

1 Use a marker to make a level cutting line around the gourd.

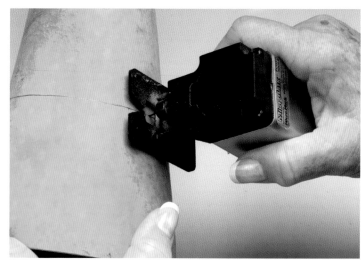

2 Use a craft saw to cut the gourd.

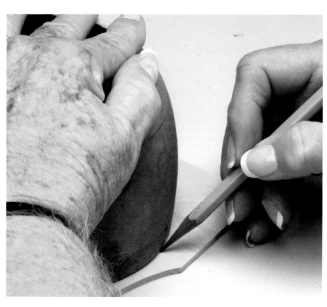

3 Draw around the gourd on the ¼" plywood scrap—put a pencil mark on the gourd and the plywood so you can match them once the cut is made.

4 Draw a second line inside the first one so that the cut circle will fit inside the gourd.

<22>

5 You want the circle to fit in the center of the gourd, allowing room at the top for the music box and room at the bottom for the key. If it's too large, cut the circle down more until it fits.

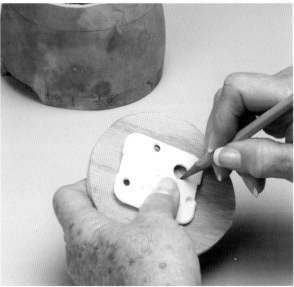

6 Remove the screws from the music box. Pop the back off and use it for a template. Mark the place for the key and screws and drill the holes. Drill a couple of extra holes for the sound to escape. Attach the music box to the plywood circle using screws ¼" longer than the original screws.

7 Position the wooden circle inside the gourd ring and glue in place.

<23>

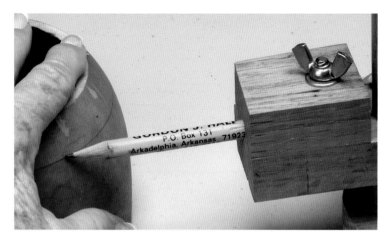

8 Turn the gourd circle upside down. Use the marker to make a line around the gourd about 1/2" up from the edge.

9 Divide the gourd into four equal sections. Measure one inch to each side of the mark and draw an arched line from the bottom of the gourd up to the pencil line.

10 Remove the section between the arches. This makes the feet and allows the music to be heard.

Painting the Base

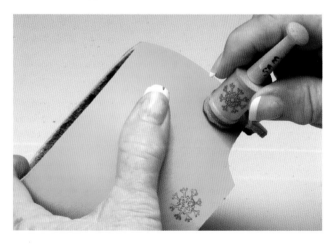

11 Use the wash brush to basecoat the gourd with Roman Stucco. Using Mocha, apply a thin layer of paint to the snowflake stamp and stamp in the center of each foot and over each arch. If you get too much paint on the stamp, blot it on a paper towel before stamping.

12 Use a chalk pencil to scribe a line above the snowflakes following the shape of the bottom of the gourd. Scribe a second line 1/8" above the first one.

<24>

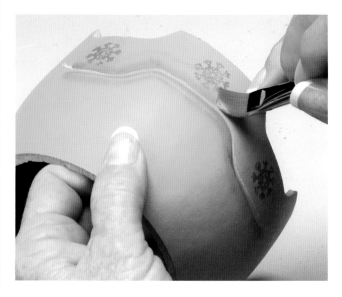

13 Use the #12 flat and Mocha to float a stroke on the outside of the chalk lines fading away from the lines. Float another stroke under the snowflakes around the bottom of the gourd fading away from the edge.

14 Trace the pattern and apply to the gourd.

15 The easiest way to apply a pattern to a round surface (and retain your sanity) is to cut it into sections and apply where needed. Place a gingerbread man above each foot and a holly berry between each gingerbread man.

<25>

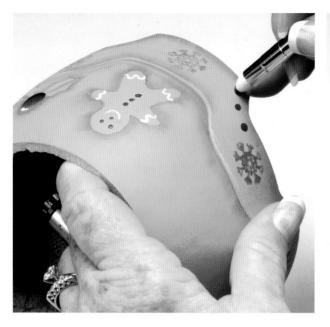

16 Float with Mocha around the gingerbread men and holly. Use the filbert brush and Barn Red to fill the holly berry in solid. Use the #12 flat to highlight the top of the berry with Deep Coral and shade the bottom with Black. Use the liner brush to place a White comma stroke across the top of the berry and for the line work on the gingerbread men. Use the berry maker to make Barn Red dots between the snowflakes and for the features on the gingerbread men.

17 Scribe a chalk line around the top of the gourd and use the liner brush with Barn Red to make a comma stroke border. Attach the base to the globe using wood glue, and allow to dry for several hours or overnight.

Painting the Globe ∼∼∼∼∼∼∼∼∼∼∼∼∼∼∼∼∼∼∼∼∼∼∼∼∼∼∼∼∼∼

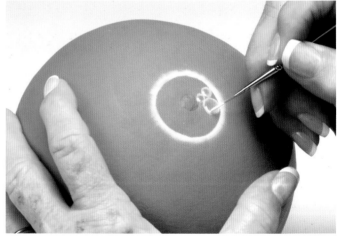

18 The sky is Cape Cod Blue and the snow is Chambray Blue. Be sure to make a hill tall enough for the snow angel maker. Use the #12 flat and White to highlight the snow where it meets the sky and float random streaks throughout the snow.

19 Use the #12 and White to float a circle fading outward on top of the globe. Paint smaller water drops fading inward inside the first circle. Use the liner brush to add White comma strokes and dots for highlight. Spatter entire gourd with thinned White to make snowfall except inside the bubble on top. Apply the pattern. Base all the snowmen in White. All the carrot noses are Bittersweet; all men are shaded with Cape Cod and have Black eyes and buttons.

<26>

Handstanding Snowman

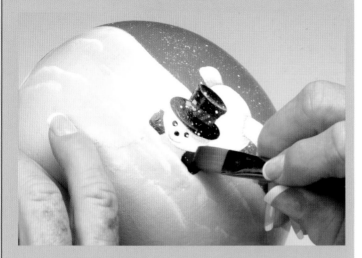

20 The hat is Black. The band is Barn Red with Deep Coral stripes. Float White around the top and along one side of the hat for highlight. The mittens are Barn Red shaded with Black.

Snow Angel-making Snowman

21 The vest is Ivory with Barn Red stripes. Float Cape Cod fan shapes around the arms and legs and then use the edge of your flat brush to add White lines.

Leapfrogging Snowmen

22 The top snowman has Opaque Red earmuffs and scarf with White stripes. Shade with Barn Red. The bottom snowman has a Deep River cap with White zigzag stripes and Opaque Red mittens. Shade the mittens with Barn Red and highlight with Deep Coral.

Ice-skating Snowman

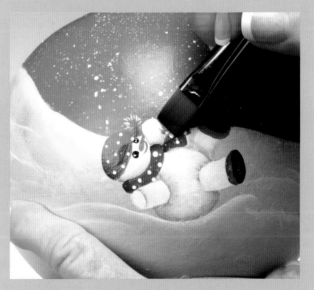

23 The skates are Mocha with Black soles. The blades are a mix of Black and White 1:1. The scarf and cap are Opaque Red shaded with Black Cherry and White polka dots. Finish with several light coats of spray varnish, but allow for drying time between coats.

<27>

Snowman Candycane Holder

Palette – Delta Ceramcoat

White • Black • Opaque Red • Tangerine •Black Cherry • Deep River Green • Blue Haze • Adobe

Brushes – Loew-Cornell

Series 7300 #12 flat shader
Series 7350 10/0 liner
Series 7500 #6 filbert
Series 7550 1" wash brush
515-L berry maker
#275 mop

Supplies

8-10" tall bottle gourd
Wood glue
3 small pom-poms
Silk sponge
Small round sponge
3' long 5/16" dowel
Drill and 5/16" bit
3/4" scrap plywood or MDF
Glue gun
Strip of fabric
Delta spray varnish
Blending gel

<28>

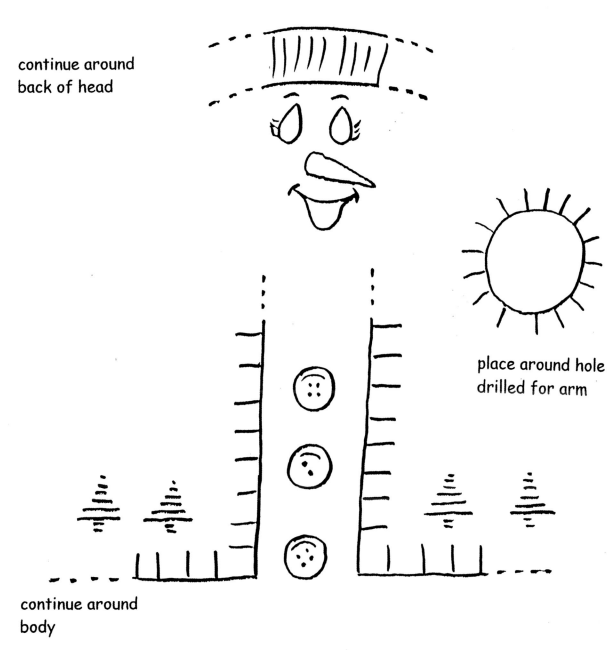

continue around
back of head

place around hole
drilled for arm

continue around
body

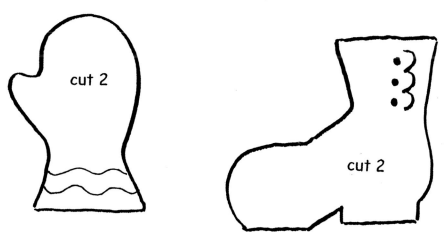

cut 2

cut 2

<29>

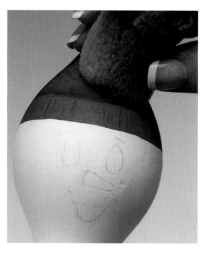

1 Use the wash brush to basecoat the entire gourd White. Using a 5/16" drill bit, make two holes in the bottom for the legs and a hole on each side for the arms. Take care to get the arm holes level with each other.

2 Apply the pattern and base the cap in Opaque Red. Shade around the brim with Black Cherry. Use the liner brush to make lines on the brim. Use the silk sponge to apply texture over the rest of the cap. Connect the earmuffs with a line of Black across the top of the cap from ear to ear.

3 Base the vest with Deep River Green. This color will take at least three coats. The stitching and design are done with the liner brush and thinned White.

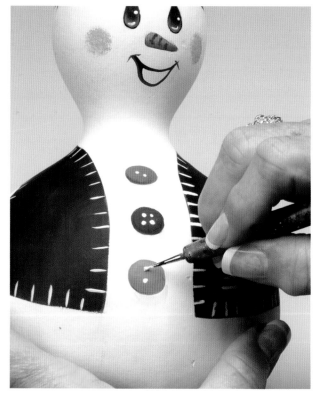

4 The eyes are Black with Blue Haze floats and the mouth is Black Cherry made with the liner brush. Apply blending gel to the cheeks and sponge on Adobe. Mop to soften if needed.

5 Paint the buttons: one Opaque Red, one Deep River Green, and one Tangerine. Shade the bottom of the red and orange buttons with Black Cherry and the bottom of the green one with Black. Shade under the buttons with Blue Haze. Use the stylus and White to make the buttonholes.

<30>

6 Cut the mittens and shoes from the plywood. Paint the mittens Deep River Green and use the liner brush to make wiggly White and Opaque Red lines on the cuffs.

7 Paint the shoes Black. Use the #12 flat and White to float a scalloped line on the outside of each shoe. Place White dots for buttons using the berry maker.

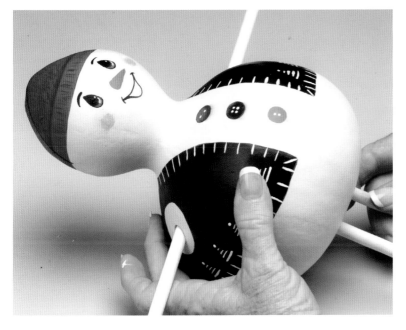

8 Cut one section of dowel 12" long for the arms and two sections 6" long for the legs. Push the arm dowel through the body and glue the mittens on with the thumbs turned up. Glue the shoes on the shorter dowels and glue them in place. Turn the toes outward to give him a better stance. If you have trouble getting him to stand, cut little skis or snowshoes out of 1/4" plywood and glue to his shoes. Spray with several light coats of varnish, allowing for drying time between coats.

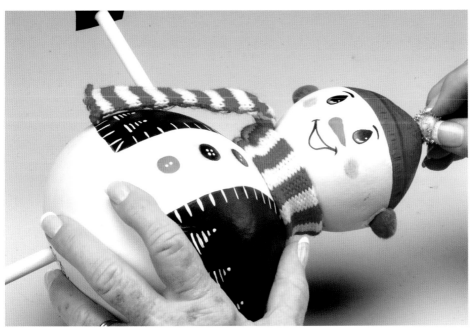

9 Glue the fabric scrap on for a scarf and glue the pompoms in place. Hang candy canes on his arms and enjoy.

Susan's Soldier

Palette-Delta Ceramcoat

Black • Bridgeport Grey • Opaque
Red •Tangerine • Ivory • Black
Cherry • White• Golden Brown
•14k Gold • Medium Flesh •Adobe
• Desert Sun • Blue Danube

Brushes – Loew-Cornell

Series 7000 #6 round
Series 7300 #2, 12 flat shaders
Series 7350 10/0 liner
Series 7500 #6 filbert
Series 7520 ½" rake
Series 7550 1" wash
515-M berry maker
#275 mop

Supplies

Bottle gourd*
Delta spray varnish
Leveling tool
Small round sponge
Glue gun
7 blue acrylic stars
Blending gel

*Any size gourd will work. Adjust the
pattern to fit.

<32>

<33>

1 Use the leveling tool to draw lines around the gourd for the bottom of the hat and the bottom and top of the jacket.

2 Use the wash brush to basecoat the hat and pants Black, the coat Opaque Red, and the face Medium Flesh.

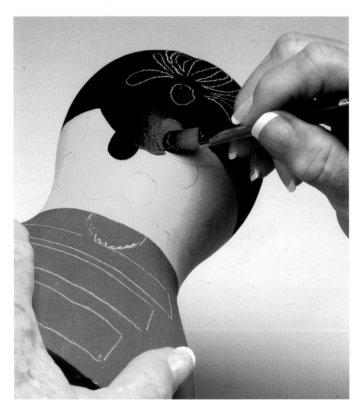

3 Apply the pattern and paint the eyes and cap brim Black.

4 Use the #12 flat and Desert Sun to float around the nose, under the brim and lip, and inside and outside the ears.

<34>

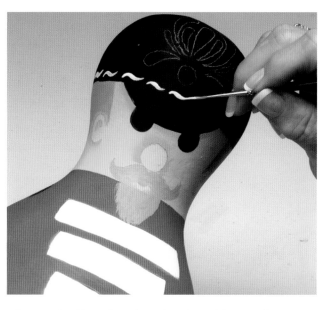

5 Use the rake brush and Bridgeport Grey to paint the hair and beard. Keep the edges ragged. Paint the bars on the coat with Ivory.

6 Use the liner brush and 14k Gold to make "S" strokes on the cap.

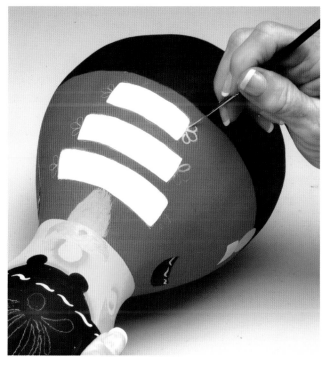

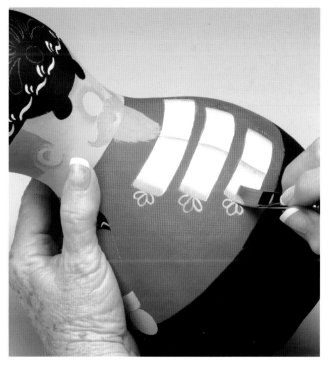

7 Use the same brush and color for the loops.

8 Use the #12 and Golden Brown to shade a line down the center and at each end of the bars.

<35>

9 Use the round brush and Opaque Red and then Blue Danube to paint the pattern on the hat. Use the #12 and Blue Danube to float around the edge of the hat brim.

10 Apply blending gel to the cheeks. Use the small sponge and Adobe to paint the cheeks. Follow with the mop brush if needed

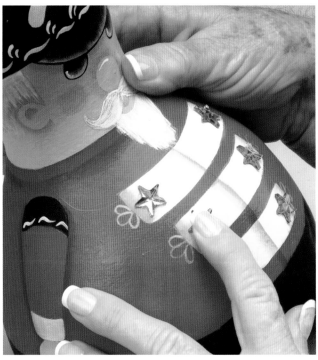

11 Use the rake brush and White to paint the hair and beard. Keep the edges ragged and leave some of the grey showing to add depth. Finish with several light coats of spray varnish, allowing for drying time between coats.

12 Glue the stars in place on the hat and the bars.

<36>

Snowmen in the Round

Palette – Delta Ceramcoat

Black • Tangerine • White
• Opaque Red
• Alpine • 14k Gold

Brushes – Loew-Cornell

Series 7000 #4 round
Series 7300 #2, 4, 12 flat
Series 7350 10/0 liner
Series 7500 #10 filbert
Series7550 1" wash
515-L berry maker

Supplies

Cannonball gourd
White chalk pencil
Toothpick
Craft glue
X-Acto knife
Delta spray varnish
Gold cord or ribbon
Craft lathe*

*Craft lathe available from Suncrest Mfg., 1387 W. 1800 N., Clinton, Utah 84015

<37>

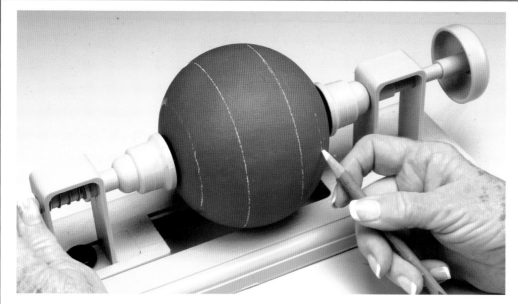

1 Use the wash brush to basecoat the entire gourd Opaque Red. When dry, place in the lathe and scribe four lines around the gourd. You may leave the gourd in the lathe to paint the lines if you like.

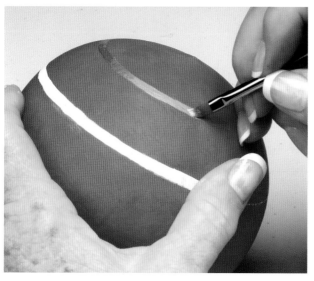

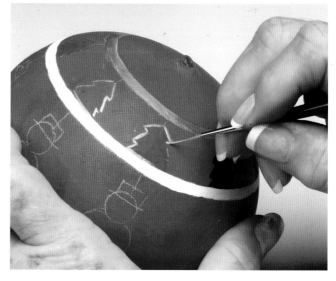

2 Use the #2 flat and 14k Gold to paint the top line around the top. Paint the next line and fill in between the two lines on the bottom with White. Use the liner and 14k Gold to line on each side of the White band.

3 Divide the gourd into four equal parts and then divide each section again. This should give you eight sections. Apply a tree pattern on each mark and paint them Alpine. Use the liner brush and 14k Gold to outline them. Use the berry maker to place gold dots between the trees.

4 Apply a snowman pattern in the wide band beneath each tree. Use the filbert brush and White to fill them in.

<38>

5 Use the liner brush and Black for the hats, buttons, arms, and features. The noses are Tangerine.

6 Use the berry maker and Alpine to place a dot under each snowman. Use the #4 flat and Opaque Red to make "S" strokes between the dots. Finish with several light coats of spray varnish, allowing for drying time between coats.

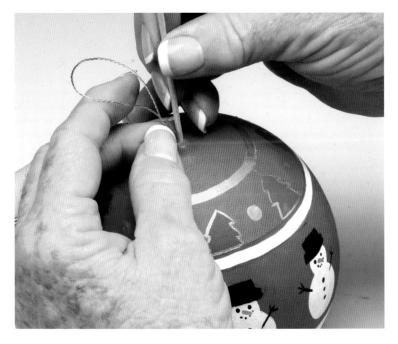

7 Make a small hole in the top of the gourd with the craft knife. Cut a length of cord and knot the ends together. Place a spot of glue on the knot and use the toothpick to push the knot into the hole. Break the toothpick off evenly with the surface and touch up with paint if needed.

<39>

Toy Soldier Snowman

Palette – Delta Ceramcoat

Bridgeport Grey • Tangerine
• Burnt Sienna • Adobe
• Black Cherry • Trail Tan
• 14k Gold • Opaque Red
• White • Black

Brushes – Loew-Cornell

Series 7300 #6, 12 flat
Series 7350 10/0 liner
Series 7500 #10 filbert
Series 7550 1" wash

Supplies

10-12" tall bottle gourd
Egg gourd
4-5" diamond club gourd
Spackle
1/2" drill bit & drill
Wood glue
3" long 1/2" dowel
Silk sponge
Craft saw* or knife
Blending gel
Fine grit sandpaper
Spray varnish
Profile tool**

*The craft saw is available from tur-
tlefeathers.net, 1-828-488-8586
** The profile tool is available at most
hardware stores.

<40>

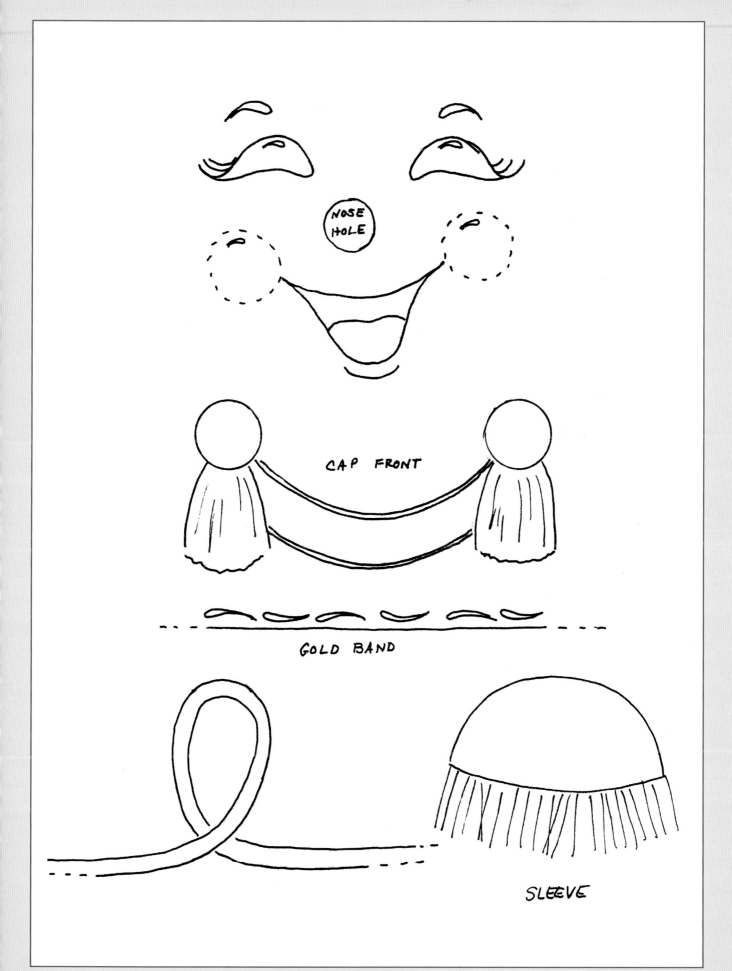

NOSE HOLE

CAP FRONT

GOLD BAND

SLEEVE

<41>

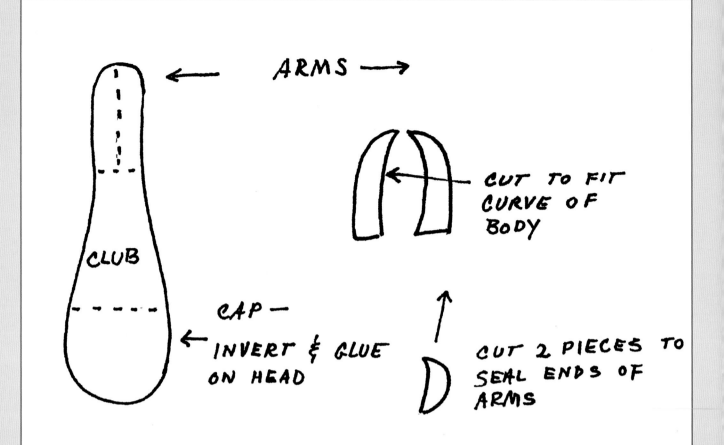

ARMS

CUT TO FIT
CURVE OF
BODY

CLUB

CAP —
INVERT & GLUE
ON HEAD

CUT 2 PIECES TO
SEAL ENDS OF
ARMS

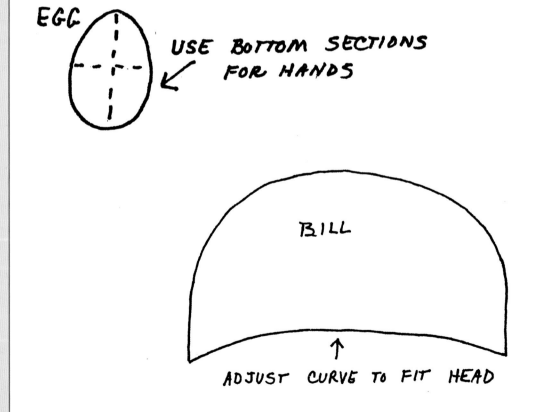

EGG

USE BOTTOM SECTIONS
FOR HANDS

BILL

ADJUST CURVE TO FIT HEAD

<42>

JACKET

FRONT

<43>

1 Press the profile tool against the gourd to make the shape for the cap's bill.

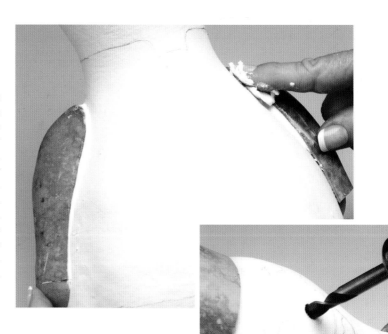

2 Hold the profile against a scrap piece of gourd and trace the shape of the bill. Use this same method to determine the shape of the arms. Use the craft saw to cut the bill and arms.

3 Glue the cap, bill, and arms in place and use tape to secure until the glue dries. Cut an egg gourd in half. Cut the half in half and glue at the ends of the arms for hands.

4 Fill any gaps with spackle. The smoother you get it now, the less sanding you will have to do when it's dry. I barely moisten my finger to remove excess spackle. Don't get your finger too wet or it will remove too much spackle. Too little water has the same effect. When you get it just right, you won't have to sand at all and the seam will be invisible. I use Dap Fast 'N Final Lightweight Spackle. It seems to dry the fastest of all I've tried.

5 Use the drill to make the hole for the nose. The dowel can be tapered using a pencil sharpener, but don't get it too sharp. Apply the pattern. Paint the dowel Tangerine and glue in place.

<44>

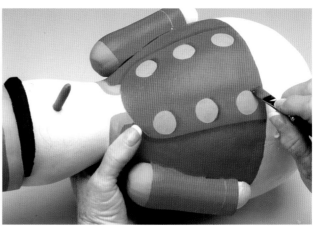

6 Use the wash brush to basecoat the cap and jacket Opaque Red. The bill is Black. All gold items should be undercoated with Trail Tan first. This will require fewer coats of gold and give you fewer streaks.

7 Use the #12 and Black Cherry to shade under the tassels, buttons, and around the jacket flap.

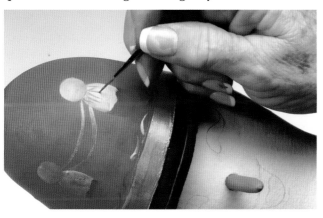

8 Use the #12 to paint the Trail Tan areas with 14k Gold. Use the liner brush to paint lines between the tassels and to paint a line of comma strokes around the cap just above the gold band. Shade the tassels and buttons with Burnt Sienna. Use the same color and the liner brush to pull lines on the tassel bottoms.

9 Use the liner brush and Black to paint the eyes, brows, and inside the mouth. The tongue is Black Cherry.

10 Apply blending gel to the cheeks and tap in some Adobe. Use the mop to soften and blend. Float a line beneath the mouth and at the top of the jacket using the #12 brush and Bridgeport Grey.

11 Use the liner brush and White to add comma strokes to the eyes and cheeks. Finish with several light coats of varnish, allowing for drying time between coats.

<45>

chapter TWO

Holiday Ornaments

Triptych Ornament

Palette – Delta Ceramcoat

Black • White • Putty
• Purple Smoke
• Raw Sienna • Maple Sugar

Brushes – Loew-Cornell

Series 730 #12 flat shader
Series 7350 10/0 liner

Supplies

4-5" cannonball gourd
X-acto knife
Hanging cord or ribbon
Ornament cap
Circle template
Glue gun
Delta spray varnish

<47>

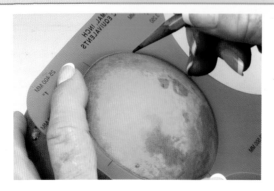

1 Use the template to draw three circles around the gourd. Draw a smaller one on top.

2 Use the #12 and Putty to basecoat the space between the circles. Use Raw Sienna to float a line around the circles 1/8" away from the edge.

3 Apply the pattern minus details and paint the sky Purple Smoke. The mountains and ground are Maple Sugar. Shade the mountains and the horizon with Raw Sienna. When dry, wash the ground with Raw Sienna.

4 Apply pattern details and paint all the figures, trees, buildings, and animals Black. Highlight with Purple Smoke.

5 The stars are made using a stylus and White. The guiding star is enhanced by using the 10/0 liner to make thin lines radiating out from the dot. Use the #12 to float around the dot, fading outward.

6 Use Purple Smoke and the berry maker to place three dots in a triangle near the top between the scenes

7 Use the X-Acto® knife to make a small hole in the top. Put the ornament hanger in place and glue securely. Finish with several light coats of spray varnish, allowing for drying time between coats.

<48>

Peppermint Santa Ornament

Palette – Delta Ceramcoat

Adobe • Black • White • Medium
Flesh • Santa's Flesh • Rain Grey
• Opaque Red • Black Cherry
• Chambray Blue • Desert
Sun • Burnt Sienna

Brushes – Loew-Cornell

Series 7300 #2 flat
Series 7350 10/0 liner
Series 7520 ½" rake
275 mop

Supplies

3 ½" round and 2 ½" round gourds
Large needle
4-5" of 1/8" ribbon
White fur
Santa hat
Glue gun
White chalk pencil
Craft lathe*
Wood glue
Blending gel
Dime (10 cents)
Delta spray varnish

*The craft lathe is available from Suncrest
Mfg.,1387 W. 1800N, Clinton, Utah 84015

<49>

1 Basecoat the smaller gourd with Medium Flesh. When dry, apply the face pattern.

ARM

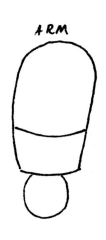

2 Outline the features with Burnt Sienna using the liner.

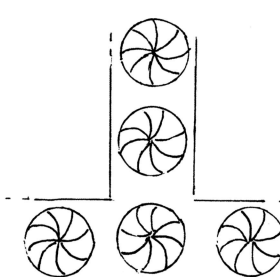

3 Use the liner brush and White to fill in the eyes entirely. This allows you to more easily see if the eyes are level and the same size. Paint the iris Chambray Blue and the pupils Black. Use the liner to place a White comma stroke in each eye.

<50>

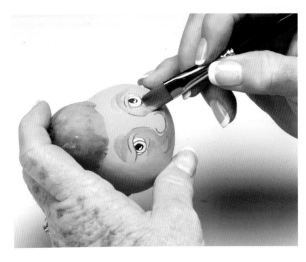

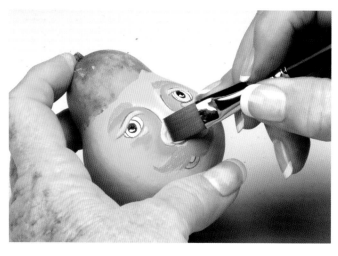

4 Use the #12 flat and Desert Sun to shade under the brow, around the nose, and under the bags beneath the eyes.

5 Use Santa's Flesh to highlight down both sides of the nose, on the eyelids, and on the bags beneath the eyes.

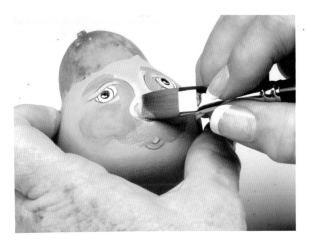

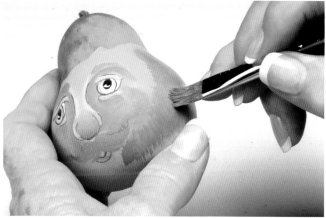

6 Apply blending gel and tap in a little Adobe on each cheek. Use the mop to soften. Float a little Adobe on the lip and the bottom of the nose, too.

7 Use the rake brush and thinned Rain Grey to fill in the moustache, brows, and hair.

8 Use the rake brush and White to repeat the last step, but leave some of the grey showing. Use the liner brush to refine the brows and moustache.

<51>

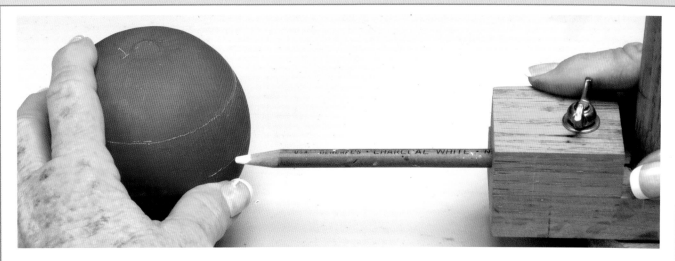

9 Basecoat the larger gourd Opaque Red. When dry, use the leveling tool with the chalk pencil to draw two lines on the larger ball with space for a dime between them. Draw two more lines from the top of the gourd down to the first lines.

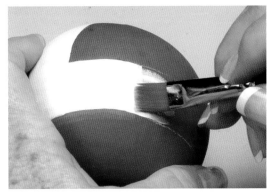

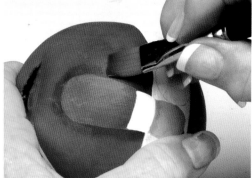

11 Apply the arm pattern and paint the cuff White, the hand Medium Flesh, and shade around the arm with Black Cherry. Shade the hand with Desert Sun.

10 Paint between all the lines with White.

12 Start in the back in case your spacing is off and draw circles all the way around the gourd on the white bands using the dime as a template. Apply the candy pattern and paint half the sections Opaque Red. Shade the white sections at the edge with Chambray Blue.

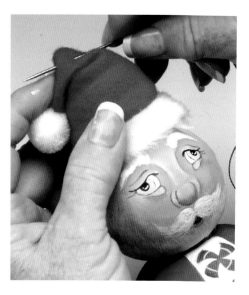

13 Use the #12 flat to shade the red sections at the edges with Black Cherry. Use the liner and White to place a "shine" on the candies.

14 Glue the two gourds together and finish with several light coats of spray varnish, allowing for drying time between coats. Glue the hat on. When dry, thread a cord or ribbon through the hat and tie the ends together to make a hanger.

<52>

Toboggan Kid Ornament

Palette – Delta Ceramcoat

Medium Flesh • Desert Sun
• White • Quaker Grey • Black •
Adobe • Opaque Red
• Deep River Green

Brushes – Loew-Cornell

Series 7300 # 12 flat shader
Series 7350 10/0 liner
Series 7500 #6 filbert
Series 7520 ½" rake
515-M berry maker
#275 mop

Supplies

Nipple gourd
Glue gun
Pompom
4-5" of 1/8" ribbon
Silk sponge
Delta spray varnish
Q-tips
Blending gel

<53>

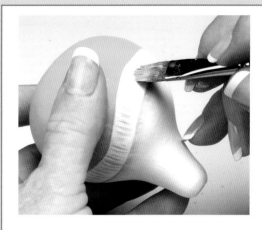

1 Apply the hat brim pattern only. Basecoat the top White and the bottom Medium Flesh. Use the #12 and Quaker Grey to float a line ½" from the edge of the white. Use the rake brush and Grey to make ribbing. Sponge Quaker Grey over the rest of the cap.

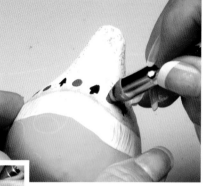

2 Starting in the back, use the liner brush and Deep River Green to make the trees around the hat. Follow with a dot of Opaque Red between each tree.

3 Apply the face pattern. Use the #12 flat and Desert Sun to float around the nose. Apply blending gel and tap in some Adobe on the cheeks. Mop to soften.

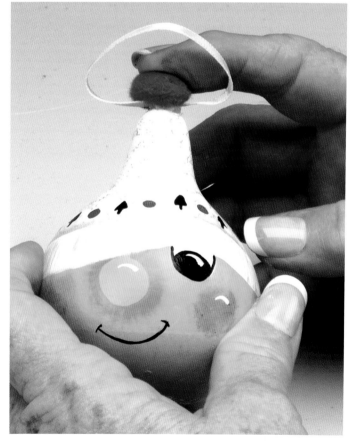

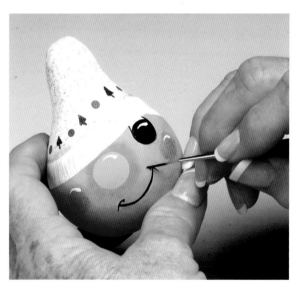

4 Using the filbert and Black, fill in the eye with White. Paint the iris Black and outline the eye and mouth with Black. Place a White comma stroke in the eye, on the cheeks, and the nose. Spray with several light coats of varnish, allowing for drying time between coats.

5 Glue a ribbon into a circle and glue to the top of the gourd. Glue a pompom inside the circle.

<54>

Winter Scene Snowman Ornament

Palette – Delta Ceramcoat

Black • Tangerine • White • Dark
Foliage • Bambi • Light Foliage
• Yellow • Chambray Blue
• Spice Brown • Opaque Red

Brushes – Loew-Cornell

Series 7300 #12 flat
Series 7350 10/0 liner

Supplies

2-3" round gourd
mushroom bird
eye screw
Twigs
Wood glue
Delta spray varnish
Nutcracker head*
X-Acto knife

* The nutcracker head is available
from Zim's,
Inc. at 1-800-453-6420

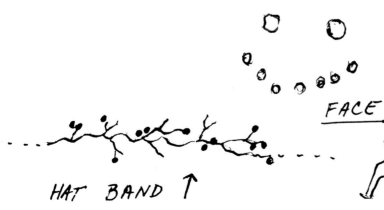

FACE

HAT BAND ↑

<55>

Painting the Head

1 Basecoat the hat Opaque Red and the head White. Use the liner brush and Bambi to paint a squiggly vine around the hat for a band. Use the stylus to place dots of White and Light Foliage on the vine.

2 Apply the face pattern. Paint the nose Tangerine and the features Black. Use the stylus to place a White dot in the eyes.

Painting the Body

3 Paint the top of the gourd Chambray Blue and the bottom White. Apply the deer and tree pattern. Paint the deer Bambi and shade with Spice Brown. There's a touch of White on the belly and under the tail.

4 Basecoat the tree with Dark Foliage. Use the liner brush to pull streaks of Light Foliage followed by White, leaving a little of each color showing.

5 Paint the birds Opaque Red and use the stylus to make Yellow eyes and beaks.

6 I didn't have a round gourd like the pattern called for, so I used what I had and cut the top off before gluing the two pieces together. Use the X-Acto knife to make small holes for the arms. Glue the twigs in place and spray with several light coats of varnish, but allow for drying time between coats.

<56>

Lifesaver Tree Ornament

Palette – Delta Ceramcoat

Light Foliage • Dark Foliage
• Custard • Butter Yellow
• Cornsilk Yellow • Calypso
Orange • Dark Goldenrod
• Butter Cream • Opaque Red
• Black Cherry • Tangerine
• Lime Sorbet • Lime Lilac
• Pale Lilac • Wisteria

Brushes – Loew-Cornell

Series 7120 ½" rake brush
Series 7300 #12 flat shader
Series 7500 #6 filbert
Series 7550 1" wash
515-L berry maker

Supplies

Extra large egg gourd
White chalk pencil
Gold star button
Toothpick
Delta Sparkle Glaze
Craft glue
Dime (10 cents)
Gold cord

<57>

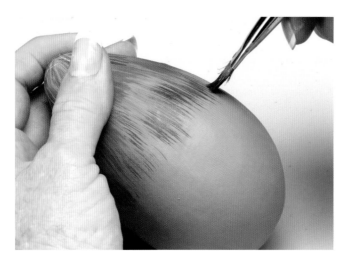

1 Basecoat the entire gourd with Light Foliage. Use the rake brush to pull lines of Dark Foliage.

2 Use the dime and the chalk pencil to draw circles all over the gourd, overlapping the rows like fish scales.

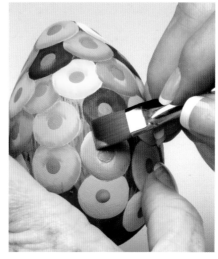

4 Highlight using Cornsilk Yellow on the yellow one, Butter Cream on the orange, tangerine and red, Lime Sorbet + White 1:1 on the green, and Pale Lilac on the Lilac. Shade using Butter Yellow on the yellow one, Dark Goldenrod on the orange, Black Cherry on the red, Lime on the green, and Wisteria on the Lilac.

3 Basecoat the circles solid using the filbert and Custard, Calypso Orange, Opaque Red, Lime Sorbet and Lilac. Use the berry maker and Light Foliage to make the centers.

5 Use the wash brush to apply sparkle glaze over the entire gourd. Use the X-Acto knife to make a small hole in the top of the gourd. Cut a length of cord and knot the ends together. Put a spot of glue on the knot and use the toothpick to push it into the hole. Snap the toothpick off evenly with the gourd and touch with paint if needed. Do NOT varnish—that will dull the sparkle finish.

<58>

Nutcracker King Ornament

Palette – Delta Ceramcoat

Opaque Red • 14k Gold
• White • Black • Rough •
Medium Flesh • Black Cherry
• Golden Brown • Ivory
• Burnt Sienna • Santa's Flesh
• Desert Sun • Storm Grey

Brushes – Loew-Cornell

Series 7300 #2, 12 flats
Series 7350 10/0 liner
Series 7500 #6 filbert

Supplies

Round tennis ball size gourd
King head #94-37A*
White rabbit pelt
Wood glue
Small eye screw
Glue gun
X-Acto knife
4 stars

* The nutcracker head is available
from Zim's, Inc. at 1-800-453-6420

<59>

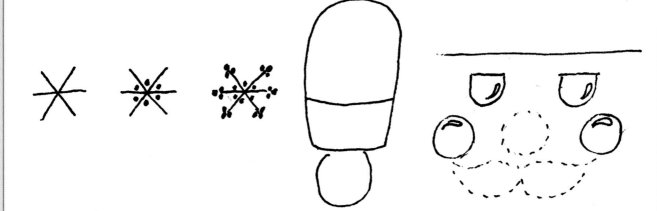

King Nutcracker Assembly Instructions

Press the brass studs into place on the bars. Measure around the head where the hair will be. Turn the fur over and mark the back crosswise of the direction the fir grows. Use the X-acto knife to cut the fur, holding it up off the surface so that nothing is cut except the hide. This eliminates chops of fur and flying hair. Butt the fur up against the bottom of the crown and glue in place. Attach the eye screw to the top of the head. Thread the ribbon through the eye screw and tie ends together.

Painting the Head

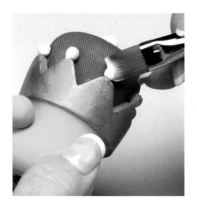

1 Paint the face Medium Flesh, the lower crown 14k Gold, upper crown Opaque Red, and the knobs and moustache White.

3 Starting in the back, use the liner brush and Opaque Red to make "S" strokes around the bottom of the crown.

2 Use the liner brush and thinned White to make a star with six arms. Use the stylus to place White dots between each line and at the end of each arm.

4 Use the filbert brush and Black to fill in the eyes. Use the #12 flat brush to float circles on the cheeks.

<60>

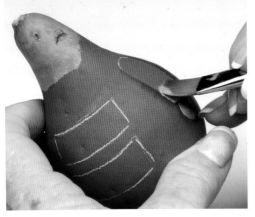

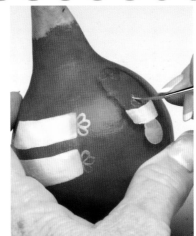

6 Use the liner brush and 14k Gold to make the loops on the sleeves and chest. Finish with several light coats of varnish, allowing for drying time between coats.

5 Apply the pattern to the body and paint the hand Medium Flesh and the cuffs and bars on the coat Ivory. Shade around the arm with Black Cherry and shade the ends of the cuffs and bars with Golden Brown.

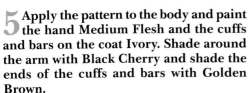

8 Hot glue the fur in place. Screw the eye screw into the top for the hanger.

7 Measure around the head beneath the crown. Mark your measurement on the backside of the pelt. (Ballpoint pen works very well for this.) Then join the two marks with a line drawn about ³⁄₄" down from the edge of the pelt.

Holding the pelt between your fingers and up off the table, use the X-Acto blade to make the cut. This eliminates cutting the fur. As you can see in the photo, you'll slightly curve the lower ends as you cut.

9 If using something other than a round gourd, cut the neck off and then glue the body and head together. Glue the stars at the ends of the bars.

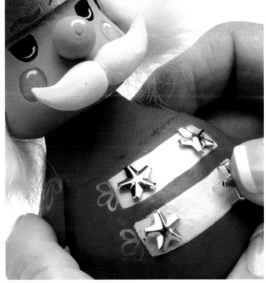

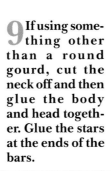

<61>

Gallery

<62>

<63>

<64>